Love Letters to the World

Also by George Genovese and published by Ginninderra Press

Time Steals Softer
The Essential Space of Play

George Genovese

Love Letters to the World

To Silke Genovese, Gill Dalton, Charmaine Newbegin,
Peggy Kimberley, Alan Pose and Alex Skovron
in appreciation of their encouragement and support.

Love Letters to the World
ISBN 978 1 76041 239 5
Copyright © George Genovese 2016
Cover painting: *Horse Woman* by Ingrid Andrew
Photograph: Marek Witkowski

First published 2016 by
GINNINDERRA PRESS
PO Box 3461 Port Adelaide 5015 Australia
www.ginninderrapress.com.au

Contents

Moonlit Glade	7
Such things…	8
Garlic	10
The Dead	11
Enmeshed	12
Anxiety	13
Dancing Wind	14
Desire without an Object	15
Drunkard	16
Leavings	17
I see two women	21
At an Untroubled Distance	22
Circumrotations around Desire…	23
Cup	24
Shell	26
A Worthless Truth	27
Table and Book	28
Waiting	30
Poem to a Check-out Girl	31
Money	32
Insider	34
The Future Lacks a Word…	35
Sleep – Return Journey	36
Meeting	42
When Women Are As Horses	43
Love Letters to the World	44
Psyche	48
Sometimes I've Sensed	49
Remembrance	51
Walking	52

Nostalgia	60
If once (my human good)	61
Omm	62
Earthing	63
Kinetic Vision	69
Barbecue	70
Seagull (Exiting Parliament Station Underground)	72
Play	74
Monolith	76
Glory days	77
Celebrity	79
Nascent	80
Villanelle	81
The Fanatic	82
Impossible Love	83

Moonlit Glade

for Alan Loney

If in this glade
there was no mesh
of lunar light
and inky leaves,

no airy way
for crystal rays
and sable deeps
to constellate

an umbral web
of twisted trees,
no chequered play
or yielding of

a clearing made
of fallen text,
then you would not
have journeyed by

this page-white light
and leafy shade,
nor happened on
a moonlit glade…

Such things…

for David Ward-Steinman

Such things I prize though most might not:

the flecks of gold that soothe the gloam
of cool arboreal canopies,
and footfalls on their freckled floors
as my stray thoughts are tinctured green;

the fragrant morning's dewy grass
profusely strewn with lustrous gems,
an open purse of proffered wealth
unseen or sought by lustful men;

and long autumnal avenues
combusting into burgundy
with saffron tongues of trembling flame
and softly rustled psalmody;

or mottled azure's purple clouds –
the sunset bleeding from its depths –
and wheeling gulls in rising gyres
aflush with crimson on their breasts;

spun filigrees of wispy mist
on foaming banks of massy moss,
and loamy-scented, mouldy bark,
by lichen-splotched and speckled rocks;

and all such actual, concrete things,
or abstract imprints on their forms,
which yield the means to flesh my dreams
and give my vision range to roam;

yes, hold them all in high esteem,
these worthless things by minted rate,
which being priceless so are free
for lawful soul and thief to take.

Garlic

Is it a kind of knowledge
that garlic cloves
unplanted in a carton
begin to sprout?

Without light, earth or water,
sensing their season?
Have they throughout the aeons
drawn earth and time

into their memories,
that even something
dark and sterile as
a human box

no way obstructs their springing?
So rooted in
their nature, may I, who
am not rooted in

my own, in earth nor in
unnumbered time,
then fairly seek their wisdom
with all such questions?

The Dead

I keep you in the silences
and meet you there,
hold you in the secret spaces none
can see we share;
to them I'm in
this barren place of sheer
appearance – alone.

When I'm at home or working, pause
a space and look
ahead (as those around me think, to catch
my breath and rest) –
I leave their land
of mere appearance, and
turn to yours instead.

Enmeshed

Encountering a spinning spider,
invention sang before itself,
outspread a syntax spun
of parallels across
the radial silks of utterance,

sang to itself its open centre, saying,
'Whether I will my web, or instinct
fashions what seems willing,
my song arrives as just this pattern,
its import: life and death.

Perhaps this song itself may be
entangled in its telling, and,
debarred exterior source or solace,
occluded in a mesh
of meaning that compels this weave,

or may, perhaps, supported as
it is by sturdy trees,
awaiting as it does the foreign food
that will sustain me, touch
on what remains beyond its making.'

Anxiety

It's not for any work or taxing bout,
you're slowly worn and whittled to the ground –
it's in the drain of worry life leaks out.

In paralysing dread and sapping doubt
the will's subdued, enfeebled, and then bound,
and not for any work or taxing bout.

It's for those snaring thoughts that stalk and scout
each waking hour's fatigued and tautly wound –
it's in the drain of worry life leaks out.

You ached for hopeless dearth and soulless drought,
the fear of what tomorrow might bring 'round,
and not for any work or taxing bout.

No strain alone erodes a soul, once stout,
but just the fretting stress a spirit found –
it's in the drain of worry life leaks out.

No ceaseless labour brought your end about
to lay you low beneath a mouldy mound,
it's not for any work or taxing bout
but in the waste of worry life leaked out.

Dancing Wind

It came a dancing wind, voiced over
horizonal lines,
skipped lithely through the pure divide
of figurative earth and sky;
it came and scuffed the sibilant grass
and with an aspirated twist,
whipped round the punctuated dunes
of rubble bricks and syllable-stone.

Glissading softly with the grammar of a hiss
or whistling fleshed to lapping waves,
it took my tongue and searching lips
and parsed my words, and with
a syntax of unruly sound,
my sense descending on its ebb,
so placed me down, a speck of sand,
and then was gone…

Desire without an Object

Were my desire spurred by a lusted goal,
harried and gnawed by hunger, mauled to the soul,
it would exploit whatever rapid means
to snare its spoil, and in its hot pursuit
run down and slay the trophy of its dreams
to gorge itself until its lack fell mute.
But weighed down by a leaden lassitude –
a saturnine paralysis – I move
in pent up circles of futility
and lack the purpose of a biting want;
confronting everywhere sterility,
an apathy that is my constant taunt,
my objectless desire finds no relief
but robs all things of value – like a thief.

Drunkard

(Q: What have an empty bottle and a full drinker in common?
A: They're both drunk.)

He was that way once: sprightly, lively, gracious,
his eyes aflame with warm and subtle fire,
his conversation sparked with friendly wit.
His was a soul both generous and spacious
before succumbing to a fraught desire
that extirpated any hope from it.
A burning paradox, this glass of liquor
applies the balm that sooths and makes him sicker,
inflames the suffering he would extinguish
yet magnifies the impotence of soul.
Morosely soused, a vessel to the brim,
he drinks on past relief to grief and anguish,
and dousing fire, desire, with liquid coal,
woos consummation with what empties him.

Leavings

The essentials packed, you come
to sort the bits and pieces
between the wall and architrave.
More than a hemisphere away
in time, that postcard from Ireland,
Christmas cards from England,
peep through or hide in a random
arrangement of serrated lines…

Before this higgledy-piggledy
array of incidental history
you wonder what to take or leave:
those German coasters, quaint
with old-world charm,
evoking the spank of heels
along the cobbles trod between
the pubs of Minden town;

or else those ticket stubs
of folk performances
in Brunswick or Albert Park,
mementos of the genius
of Anglo-Gaelic artistry,
the strains of fiddles or guitars
on distant summer nights
astounding us with flights of poetry
from the likes of Hayes or Fox;

or then those paper scraps
you've long intended to decode,
enigmas written like
love letters to yourself amid
distraction or drunken reverie,
self-defeating as mnemonic notes
for what remain illegible scrawls,
yet in a sense expressions
of fidelity to the fleeting tempo of
untranslatable thought;

or else that homemade butterfly,
its cardboard body cut
from an old fruit box, its yellow wings
and orange spots, made by
a friend who in her days
of dark self-searching found
a moment's bright respite,
and tried to fix a happy hope
to a lasting metamorphosis;
already dead two years by her
own hand, this image redefines
that act and its intent
as something ambiguous, disturbing,
as if it were a premonitory
attempt at staving off the dread
of her impending demise.

So what to take or leave?
For now you make a choice
afforded by a dawdling sense of luxury –
the chance to leave aside selection and
defer decision, scoop the too-hard heap
into a box to ponder at your leisure, later,
and wonder then which memorabilia
you might decide to keep…

The house you come to settle in
was hastily vacated, abandoned
by the heavy smoking vendor
whose drink-logged body packed
it in from diabetes and self-abuse
to finish in a nursing home.

So here you are amid a mass
of things: old *Women's Weekly*s, *Playboy*s,
mechanical and military magazines;
letters from nieces and nephews
strewn amongst beer coasters
of Foster's, Courage and VB,
photographs of people in spaces
you'll never know or share,
nor the unspoken narratives
the figures in the frames withhold…

If nothing else, the irony isn't lost:
deferring personal selection, now
you're forced to sift through memories
that aren't your own – and something else
beyond mere irony, a lacerating pang
of common loss provoked by
this morass of foreign debris.
Denied his option of a choice
or chance for a deferred selection
at a later time, a merciless sense
of enforced foreclosure
hangs sullenly over all his things.

Confronted by these leavings,
you feel amid the cluttered silence
the fatally chimerical nature
of each discreet deferral, hear
it seems, dry whispers, sere
and sallow as the rustling papers
which you sort about to hiss
before a final gasp or cough:
'The way of all's surrender,
surrender willingly achieved,
or implacably imposed.'

I see two women

I see two women in my middle-age,
young as I once was, both as certain of
what life affords in its beneficence,
a life of sureties and a future of
fulfilled desire projected inevitably –
how sweet the wholesome lustre of their hair,
how fine the radiance of their youthful skin –
desire projected stubbornly again…

Is there regret in this? Nostalgia, or
a nagging loss of opportunity?
There is a feeling of distance from myself,
a sense that someone else appropriates
my memories as mine begin to thin,

as if an aged man here hidden in
my midst were standing at a slanted door
and peering in the darkness he's about
to enter, and who turns then for a moment
towards a middle-aged man who fixes on
two youthful women indistinctly glimpsed,
obscured and farther set in space from him.

At an Untroubled Distance

Waking from thirsting sleep to get a drink,
you feel it ended long ago, this dream
you live. Already you watch it from a
great distance as your body automatically
steers itself into the moonlit kitchen.
Not altogether indifferent but detached,
not desolate, but surgically observant,
some other floating self looks on the play
of mind and body in their interaction,
knows in advance the sure mechanics they
enact, the intricate exchange between
reflexive stimulus and response, and sees
the same replayed comportment through which it
remains unmoved despite your parching thirst.
Bathed in the moon's bone-smooth and sterile glow,
somewhere between a sense of liberation
and bemusement, ultimately unconcerned,
you calmly see yourself – already dead.

Circumrotations around Desire…

To see something without obstruction,
a gaze must make itself invisible;
the more things seem to draw it in
their orbit – their allure, the more
evasive must this gaze become.

So too desire, blind to itself
in its extension into vision,
divested as the longed-for object,
reveals itself as something other
through just its own misrecognition.

But when, distorted as an other,
intention fails to match its object,
desire suspects a native error,
and seeing through its failed conflation
retrieves itself as self-creation.

Cup

for Peter and Noriko Accadia

As a memorial of thirst
and will-to-satiety,
desire materialises
as this ceramic cup.

Here, with its figurative lip,
the hollow passage of
a throat that guides the drink
it draws into the faint

suggestion of a gut,
it makes of lack a place
where quenching liquid gathers,
transforming vacancy

into a brimming site
of manifest retention
where, folded in its hold,
there gleams a limpid plenum.

And yet, exceeding any
cup's capacity
or bracing metaphor's
implied ability

for semantic gathering
or symbolic succouring,
this vessel filled to fullness
can't be confluent with

fulfilled desire, as can
no substituting image
or adumbrating figure.
Its depth too vast to be

contained in visible form
or lineated measure,
desire remains the spring
from which all images flow;

and so this cup, afloat
and vaguely shimmering
on the elusive motion
of its dark current, is not

that which exists because
it satisfies a lack,
but as a lack appears
through that which vanishes…

Shell

A snail's shell
folded on
a steadfast stillness

curves from dark
interiors to
a calcareous gloss.

A radiant spire
of creative hunger
from a secret source,

it swelled around
the columellar
that held a mollusc on

its axial coil
to leave a husk
and absent chamber.

No longer drawing
a sea-world's succour,
no more projecting

a helical course,
it is this skeletal
shadow and echo

of atrophied desire,
its intricate labours
and expended force.

A Worthless Truth

An emptiness at times benumbs my senses
such that my world seems less than misty air,
and all things drained of substance, mere pretences,
lack even force to stir a faint despair…
I wonder then if all our diligence,
our earnest toil and sweat for valued goals,
all striving art, philosophy and science,
the ceaseless industry of human souls,
are nothing more than ploys we deftly use
to help divert us from a tragic farce,
and we, the players of this cunning ruse,
who desperately clutch at welcome masks,
so never sense the guile which we've employed,
disguising that, in fact, we mask a void.

Table and Book

Art is an excess of desire,
as is the simplest ornament,
the soul surfeited of its needs
craves more than mere utility

or even bodily attainment.
This useful table serves my needs
with easy practicality,
but it's the rough hewn finials

and fluted legs that lure my gaze
to meditate on art and beauty.
It's maker had a lack appeased
by these adornments, felt an urge

for pleasures taken in the touches
that go beyond plain use and function.
The book that's open on this table
shares in its way this same abundance:

the florid border on its front,
its title gilded and embossed
with variegated types of font,
all tend towards a pleasing balance

excessive of the textual sense.
And yet, its contents too accord
with this exceeding tendency,
for this book's of that curious type

that lacks a glib transparency,
nor yields a discourse that imparts
a crop of useful information
or easily digested facts.

It is a book of prodigies,
vast tangents veering into tracts
of sheer intangibility,
a book of spacious darkness pricked

with sudden flashes or a dim
and distant luminosity,
upon whose open page there reads,
'She walks in beauty, like the night…'

Waiting

My longed-for,
something of your essence stays
here fragrant, faint,

but not as you the absent
in your invisible state.
My longing's lack

is actual desire's desiring,
the act that is itself
its felt-for end.

Oh phantom absence,
present here
as self-creation's

manifested lack,
desire's supreme illusion –
for which I wait.

Poem to a Check-out Girl

That lingering look in her eyes and of mine,
the shy fascination of hesitant smiles,
delaying, though slightly, the transient – yet,
held longer than sanctioned by safe etiquette.

A strange contradiction, as I fumble my change,
this cool masquerade of commercial exchange,
when we are still churning on an intimate wake
and could, if enabled, so soften its ache.

But scanners are beeping, the registers ring,
the patron beside me arranges her things,
our moment departs us (my shopping bags filled)
with bitter-sweet poetry – and we unfulfilled.

Money

An approximate expression of
desire condenses here as money,
circulates the hidden heart's
invisible economy –
its inexact, unique demands –
and by this common currency
allows its dark asymmetries
an interappetitive exchange.

Encoded in the effigies
that mutely peer at me from money,
the double gaze of my desire
seductively twines (symbolically)
affectively invested value
with palpable numeric counts,
conflates the celebrated faces
of respectable icons with

an absolute panoptic Eye
by whose unquestioned sanction and
approved authority, this gaze
adopts conferred locality
within a hierarchy of power.
And just as power implies one
kind of desire among a scale
of others, an impetus that craves

attainment of the longed-for goals
specific to itself, as does
a man's desire to rule another
or instinct's urge to vanquish lack,
so too desire might be conceived
as just another guise for power –
a field where vying plays of sway
of relative intensity

upon a scale from weak to strong,
(attracting, shunting, shifting, colliding)
mould the contours of a psyche
in its unceasing tug o' war,
such that desire and power, being
two sides of the same coin, denote
the same relentless naked force –
in money, unmistakably so.

Insider

The invisible is in the Gaze,
its visions buoyed
on what remains withdrawn.

Desiring through what can
be shown the more
of what cannot, it sets

its sight to images held
for vision's all,
as if these could denote

that where it faintly falls
it fully forms
without an imageless death.

The Future Lacks a Word…

The future's always not-here-now
whichever way you w*end*,
not what you see, a memory,
nor even where it'll t*end*.

Not 'that' or 'then', the 'this' or 'when',
the morrows you int*end*,
but rather just what is surpassed
and lacks a captured ( )

Sleep – Return Journey

Beyond these sullen crags where furrows spread
like gashes over a disfigured land
and mournful tarns of stagnant tears collect
to fester darkly on a face of sand,

monotonous waters weep through stolid rock,
and creeping weakly in each shallow bed,
enact the movement of a thwarted passion
that trickles through an enervated head…

And here, sere bushes in a scribbled mesh
are tangled echoes of contorted thought,
and in their cryptic scrubby script encode
some vague essential secret dearly sought.

And farther still, beyond the margins of
this wilderness where stands a host of trees,
there once, amid that lush and verdant wood,
a blissful child sat toying at his ease.

Beneath a chequered canopy of gold,
he dallied with the strange inhabitants there,
the hermit meditating in his hut,
a young girl, beautiful, with flaxen hair,

and all the fearless creatures, then his friends,
would meet him where a mighty river runs,
and teaching him the wisdom of their ways,
came bearing secrets in familiar tongues.

For once he had the power to transform
himself into a bird or beast or fish –
to glide the swells of eagle-heights, or plum
the surging river with a salmon's swish!

And everything and everywhere was still
alive and softly flushed with wholesome youth,
nor was there then the blemish of a lie,
but only beauty in its naked truth.

But now that hermit, long since gone, so stoops
transfigured here into a withered tree,
his twisted limbs outstretched in mute appeal
before a deaf and sterile eternity.

And that young girl so bountiful in love,
in whose embrace he'd lay in drowsy trust,
has now become this hard and fissured stone
that slowly weathers to a crumbling dust.

And were he now to touch her as he did,
when once they played along that river's verge,
he'd stir a darkness dreaming in its murk
from which a brood of vermin would emerge…

But there, upon that hermit-tree, a snake
half-coiled and basking in its sunny bliss,
extends a flicking tongue, and scenting him,
appears to greet him with a curious hiss.

How strange and beautiful it drapes upon
that tree, its charcoal body glimmering,
its underbelly tinged a vegetable green,
with piercing eyes intently fixed on him;

whose silky body, fluid in its sheen
and careless grace, composed in languid ease,
all seem to hint of somewhere he might find
the succour for a parching thirst's release.

The snake extends, drawing its forepart up,
and with a lazy twist turns to the west,
then, as if lapping moisture from the air,
imbibes its fill, then falls again to rest.

In that direction skies are flickering, violet,
and fructifying bolts of lightning sound
across the bare expanse; he scents a hint
of rain already impregnating the ground

and turns to where the snake lay coiled about
the tree to see the twisted remnant of its slough;
surprised, and yet serenely poised, he knows
the meaning of this change and so sets off

towards the snaking lightning in the west.
How long he walked he could not clearly say,
for how is distance measured in a dream?
He only knows that gradually the way

transforms from barren rock and tracts of thistle
to one of growing grass and greenery
until he sees small foraging creatures darting
into and out of abundant shrubbery.

And suddenly, some paces more, he steps
into a verdant land of heavily laden trees
where at his feet lay pools of limpid water
to which he falls exhausted on his knees...

He drinks that cool fresh water lately fallen
as though in bowed thanks-giving on the turf,
a liquid manna drunk until, refreshed,
he hears the nearby roar of pounding surf.

He rises, charmed by the sounding sea,
its singing mingled with a moaning soft
and saline breeze, and sees ahead high dunes
fringed with a screen of shrubs, through which each waft

approaches him in scented cadences.
He mounts the sandy mounds and parts the veil
of greenery, agog before the scene;
for there, amid the nascent eve, clouds sail

a sky suffused with hues of subtle rose
which, daubed with muted mauve and bleaching blues,
outspreads in one immense, unbroken line;
and there the fluting water glitters, moves

like metal tinctured by the sulphurous sky,
its waves delighting in a nuptial dance
of partnered parts, their play a host of eyes
that draw him, giddily, into a trance.

But sovereign of the scene in majesty
the sun, emerging from the clouds, descends;
the sky, a trailing mantle in its wake,
begins to fade the farther down it bends

its mesmerizing way; down-going, down
to the horizon spins its fiery fall
and watching it he feels an awe for that
pure source of self and soul and heart of all…

And now his heart, a-thump with laughing joy,
appears to him as just a splintered spark
of that undying sun, a minute ember shot
with ecstasy into the growing dark.

With one exultant leap and one great cry
he stumbles down the dunes towards the shore,
stripping his clothes exuberantly as
he runs to meet the ocean's deafening roar!

Once there he plunges in the rolling waves
and feels the purifying bite of brine
in its suffusion of his trembling skin,
and he, renewed, refreshed this second time,

and captive to the dipping sun's descent
into an underworld of tidal night,
is ineluctably drawn along its circuit
into a nether realm beyond all trace of light;

and there, suspended in profoundest silence,
extinguished of all conscious sight and sound,
from out unbroken embryonic darkness,
the sun rekindles in its genescent round.

The nadir crossed, ascending vivified,
he feels a tidal shift assert its sway,
his senses melding with the growing light,
he's ushered to another radiant day,

and so returning from oblivious night
into his body as the morning breaks,
he runs a dry tongue along his salty lips,
a hand across his grainy eyes – and wakes.

Meeting

We went along a bridge of air
to those we held innately near,
and we, in shared symbolic code

transmitted to the aerial ear,
achieved the way's perfected end
at which we stood on solid land.

When Women Are As Horses

for Yvonne Adami

When women are as horses,
their breath suspended in
the early frigid air,
and with long pony-tails
that smell of earth and hay
they go clip-clopping in
high heels, their haunches taut
and tired as draying mares,
and when they're harnessed in
brassieres, or saddled by
the shoulder bags that leave
their prints as red as whips,
I see the burdened beast
who looks askance with wide
and whitened eyes at me
and then all dreams – ideals –
romance – dissolve in streams
of sweat along their backs.

Love Letters to the World

They are a kind of lover's letter – though
it's not essential who my lover is,
nor even if they're born yet, eager for
these words. They come from an intrinsic faith
in timeless meaning, an intent compelled
to reach another who knows just what I mean
by meaning, and affirms the same faith too.
Epistles such as this, eternal one,
are indirect appeals to those who'll help
me draw the essence of my sense with me,
a sense that could in no way manifest
without a shared and native sympathy.

As I sit here alone and write in silence,
the light-bulb crackling overhead, the world
asleep except for moths that patter at
the pane, or crickets chirping out the back,
I know whatever insight might emerge
from such nocturnal sessions must return
to me as from a far and foreign shore,
and surely, like divided friends who've long
lived overseas, but suddenly return,
arrive with that uncanny air of being
once comfortably familiar but now strange.

Whoever you may be now reading this,
my latest letter, know that in a true
and fundamental sense it's really you
who instigate this correspondence between
us; I say this because for me, at least,
it's you who must remain the goal to which
my words aspire if they're to be at all
authentic; you, my distant reader, through
whose eyes my language is compelled
to groom itself with diligence and care.

In this I'm strangely other to myself
(as strange, perhaps, as I appear to you)
for like you, I become a reader as
I write. If even just in my mind's eye,
I nonetheless attempt to scrutinise
and translate your reactions to my thoughts.
Is that a ripple on your brow there now
and what's it mean? Do these reflections cause
you puzzlement, amusement or ennui?
And is that smirk incipient scepticism
or tacit nod to textual comradeship?

To be clear, though, it's not just you whom I
address, but rather that exceeding you,
the you to which you too must always defer:
that you of word to which you're too a servant,
that you of speech through which we all refer,
that you of text whose message is concealment,
that you of sense whose essence is unsaid,
that you of sound whose music is excelling,
that you of sign whose gesture is unread,
that you of tongue whose giving is reception,
that you of silence borne beyond the song…

For let me say then, what's essential in
our meeting is the absent other who
remains removed from us, and, being so,
persists as the custodian of our saying;
the one to whom and through which language aims
but never manages complete attainment,
that one by whom we fall outside ourselves
and, paradoxically, facing the alien,
return to what is common to us both –
our being here revealed as for an other…

A barking dog curtails my reverie.
Outside, the stealthy morning thickens to
a hinted tint of twilight… But that dog,
still barking in a yard, commends himself
to something in the dying night. Like me,
he trustingly appeals to something that
would take his vocalisations for its own
and yield it back to him as understood,
something or someone like another dog,
or man or unspecific ear which in
this case is mine – yes, me his plaintive bark
addresses with its pregnant sense. There can't
be anything more foreign to that dog
(unknown to me) than me, nor I to him,
and yet I know that bark attests to his
displeasure at his lot in that backyard,
that he hurts, being lonely, needy for
affection and regard – in human terms,
quite simply, that he longs for love. 'I hear
you dog and understand – ours, cognate tongues.'

Psyche

Once, even to the ecliptic, Psyche reigned,
her reach extending to the zodiac,
as those pale vestiges of mythic glyphs
of man and animal attest. But now

depleted, shrunken to a mortal net
of neurons sealed inside the human head,
she will no longer tread incarnate through
the visible earth – not as a deity

or even fleshed in elemental shape –
for these days that denotes pathology,
a sickness wreaked on those possessed of old
poetic eyes. An anorexic shade

of former splendour and voluptuousness,
her new-found votives now, efficient technicians,
would never ask, 'But where could Psyche, seat
of revelation, ever end or start?'

Extruded from the world's diurnal light,
her old domain withdrawn, usurped by Reason,
she's banished from the scope of natural sight
and sunken to the blackest heart of matter.

And yet, though hidden, starved of eminence,
she still exerts the subtlest influence,
for, reasserting her inscrutable sway,
atomic quanta waver in her presence.

Sometimes I've Sensed

Sometimes I've sensed a moment open outward
from the depths within itself; as if
one viewing through a door, ajar, had caught
a sudden glimpse of something hidden in
one's midst – an unattended garden, so
anonymously close, till then unseen,
the curious gaze alights on with surprise…

Then, through that lovely view, one's vision roams
a hinted path as it insinuates
its winding way through overhanging flora,
meanders through obscure, circuitous heights
to disappear into the verdant deeps
that lead that moment far outside itself.

And at such times I've sensed that where an eye
would fail, stopped short by what was simply seen,
or where a mind curtailed by what was known
fell baffled, blind, before the scene it gleaned,
a vaster sense of being continued through
invisible spaces nonetheless still there,
that all that could be seen and said could not
lay bare a moment simply lived, just as
the sum of worldly things could not expose
its truth or else exhaust what could exist…

And at such times it seemed the other side
of what was seen was turned away beyond
this side of seeing, beckoning from a point
where image merged into invisibility,
or where a baffled sigh, unable still
to form a word, was taken up by silence,
and then, and only then, a tongue upon
those bluffs of silence sought the footing of
the farthest word from which to spring
and leaping blindly launched itself in song.

Remembrance

I lived you in a day-long dream,
and held you with a sleeping hand,
you were with me as gentle air
and true as earth beneath my feet.

We spoke of much but little said
through years that seemed a handful days
yet still meant more than merely words
through all our talk on darkling eves.

And they were strange, familiar too,
those open spaces where we met,
sheer distances where we traversed
the nearness of each new farewell.

We here, and there, and still to be,
could not in truth believe in loss,
unless, of course, we chose to lose
the gain of losing's press again,

for futures always came as gone,
the past returned as present, then,
and presence turned to futures now
to find past future's sudden when.

So waving you with words of love
I sailed off in my voiceless sleep,
to see myself repeat once more
recalling's echo call – a wake.

Walking

(for Julie Brennan)

Under a bowl of open blue,
a drifting shard or two of cloud,
I trundle on the gravel of
an old grey path and listen to
the sound of footfalls smack the dust;
their steady falling scrunch and scuff,
the slide and slur of sheenless shoes,
a threadbare hiss of thirsty grass
with thistles hot wind whistles through;
and then a loud cicada's drone,
the buzz of bees, a summery thrum,
the rise and fall of feet to join
and form this walking metronome.

And in a kind of swinging dance,
a dazzled stupor's rocking roll
each step discovers its own place
and falls to fold into a flow,
a flow where thought and time and space
revolve into a hazy trance,
and I, the world, my tapping feet,
this nuisance fly upon my cheek,
all melt and meet in one embrace;
while there before my downcast blur
the grand mosaic at my feet
unfolds beneath a spellbound stare.
There go the twigs, the leaves and stones,

a dying moth and cracked gum pods,
a jagged rim of Styrofoam,
some crinkled foil and plastic tops;
there go the butts of cigarettes,
a yellow fringe of sweet soursob,
a corrugated iron fence,
and an old discarded piece of cloth;
here comes a battered soft-drink can,
a sachet of tomato sauce,
a plastic straw, some twisted nails,
a long-forgotten headless bolt…
Now there what's that? I'll pick it up –
a copper penny, no it's not!

My eyes adjust and seize instead
a flattened old beer-bottle top.
But then before I know or care,
before I think to start to stop,
it fuses in the rhythm of
the flowing stream of floating things
that glide beneath my walking feet.
So on I go and on I weave
the passing vision my eyes meet
and down a wavy open road
I watch a wending memory.
But now the busy, scuttling ants
suggest a kind of secret sense

for in their lines of urgency,
their courses scurried purposely,
their movement seems to flesh the pace
and motion of my teeming thoughts.
Revolving round what could denote
the dead-fly-centre of my soul,
meandering and folding on themselves
in restless rearranging dots,
they tug and tear the fragments of
the body of their generous corpse.
And as they run, and as I go,
as what becomes escapes beyond
my vision's hold, I witness here

along the uncertain circle of
perception's corridor no break
between the inner paths of thought
and this adjacent asphalt road,
make no distinction from the ants
and me, the dirt and fly, but see
the taking up and letting go
of thought and object, thing and sight,
the constant course of lost and found
within a self-communing flow…
And in a sudden flashing flap
of iridescent wings, the whir
and slap of air and jagged caws

that jolt me from my trance-
like blur, a flock of crying crows
takes flight. And then, as if to echo
the circle of my broken thought,
their black forms tinged with sky-blue tones,
they rise to scribe above my head
a vast majestic arc. I stop!
In silence stop…and listen…hear
the soft wind slice the grass…feel it
revolve around my ankles, lift
an airy limb around my calves and thighs,
corkscrew across my back and chest
and with a twisted tongue roll round

to lick my naked neck; I close
my eyes and that soft wind descends
into an all-embracing hush,
and with its fall the movement of
my mind in its attunement to
the moment sees me fall as though
I were a raindrop plopped into
a tranquil pond, my edges fused
and lost within its vaster bounds.
Not even now a tremor where
I dropped, I have dissolved and merged
into the smoothened pond and for
a blissful moment am no more

than just its still and glassy surface…
A far off cry arouses me and then
I see those silhouetted crows
trace out a course across the sky;
as if they were a piece of wire,
they warp and spiral, twist and twang
within the heights above… I look
on down the vanishing road into
the shimmering distance, know as I
approach that point I'll only toil
to reach a goal that opens up
another distance to be crossed…
I raise a foot and let it fall.

Again the slap and tap, the crunch
and crack of gravel starts to groan
as though it were a dusty throat
and it's not long before I fold
into the same hypnotic state.
Under a colonnade of gums I go
and through a chequered tapestry
of light and shade, of flitting flecks
and stippled rays of green and gold
that shower me as though I were
a sparrow's egg, and as I do,
I feel as if my body daubed
with mottled light were nothing but

the lightness of a running beam.
At last I've got my rhythm back
and ramble with a careless step
along this rolling track. What ease
there is in this, the mindless motion,
the graceful pace and soft momentum
with which one foot recedes another,
and from its backward point, arches
its heel and rolls along its ball
to pivot for a final spring
upon an automatic toe.
And now I have a memory,
a vague remembrance of when I

still crawled, of how I looked upon
those elders in my midst
and felt against all fear of falling
an irresistible urge to stand
like them. With all the knowledge of
the human ages in my cells to aid
me in my goal, a time arrived
and marked my moment of ascent.
And though I see now through the mist
of distance, or perhaps deceive
myself and just imagine this,
it seems to me I still recall
the sweet triumphant majesty

of those first clumsy steps, recall
all those who loved me urging me
with outstretched arms until I reached
their fingertips, and after this,
my first real journey, fell into
the arms of home. Ah, what a joy
that surely was, that first attempt
of what I do with thoughtless ease
as I traverse this track with thoughts
of home – this upright movement on
two legs whose alternating shift
of weight and counterpoised imbalance
resolves into a gliding gait.

This human way of locomotion,
as defining as a hand, or speech,
or as the crowning jewel of all,
the human mind uniting this
unique creation into self-
reflected thought, unfolding each
new revelation, world and goal;
that finds itself as just the things
it senses, yet itself remains
no thing – beyond – a witness of
a world that manifests as its
own comprehension of that world,
effacing itself in each perception

and cleaving into conscious and
unconscious action, prisms of
spectral expression refracted, to
return as its own boundless question
and mirrored through its native way
of looking see itself once more...
I look up, try to recollect
the sequence of what I just thought...
its gone... I wonder if I've reached
that far, imagined point I gazed
at when I stopped before? Ahead
I only see horizon stretch
upon horizon, while to my mind's

bewilderment, reflection on
reflection follows on each tread;
reflections and horizons and
so much unfolding track to go,
more so because it's not just me
who walks along this way through time
and space, alone, but also all
who've crossed to steer this moment to
to its realisation of itself in me,
the countless souls of ages past
who've joined to form this being I am,
all them and those of ages still
to come who tread this track with me.

Nostalgia

This wafted plume,
a corolla's aura
of a passed perfume,
recalls a time's
suspended radiance;

returned in bloom
as a sudden presence,
your past extends
a fleet bouquet
distilled to an essence.

If once (my human good)

It's you who bring my heart,
draw it out so gently.
In a world of the alien head,
the face with insect eyes,
to say 'humanity' like we do,
as if that meant a boundless good
is vanity and misnaming.

But not with you because
just there, if once, it's true,
with you arrives my human good.
If once, drawn through the rift
of eyes, my heart for sake
of you allows of love enough,
then such is truth – and my truth love.

Omm

You still recall her radiant face.
She might as well have been the moon
rising over the cot's horizon.
But then,
no sun, no moon as yet took place
and she herself, no object in no room.

She was a shining presence
and when she smiled, you smiled too,
understood and smiled in her,
smiled for no displacement
or distance:
when she smiled she smiled as you.

Earthing

The human almost means a world
synonymous with earth's recession –
but earth abides.

This path long laid for human use,
the ground beneath unsettled, levelled,
cleared to an evenness and uniformity
for a foot's forgetfulness of progression,
displaces earth as far as possible
for human intention and mobility.

In what has been removed, allowed,
the hardness of its composition,
the path bespeaks the goals of swiftness,
permanence, ease and utility –
but earth abides.

The signature of the hand that held a trowel
and swept across the man-made stone
to leave its curlicues
of crisply new-laid concrete
is now no longer sensed by what is thrown
along its forward path.
Through little more than passing feet,
the caress of air and rain,
that maker's hand's reclaimed
and blunted to oblivion;
nightly snails retrace and scrawl
the earthing's iridescent monogram.

And cracks along this path,
born of the earthing's secret spasms,
the slabs of concrete buckled from
its upward thrust of roots below,
open a way for groping grass
to claw its way into the human, draw
that world back to its displaced ground.

Along its margins, olive drab
and subtle browns,
pale green and coppery splotches
of lichen lodge in minute holes
where specks of soil
have settled in the man-made stone,
allow it to take root and grow,
find nutrient and food and feed off concrete.

And where milk-thistle climbs through gaps
between the path and gutter,
gutter and road, the ideal margins that
delimit one functional zone from another,
the earthing splays those margins of occlusion
and straddles a space that is its own.

The cyclone fence ahead, still sturdy, staunch
in its occluding function
betrays nostalgia for its origins;
upon its basal shaft weep bands
of rust around the clinging wire
that hold fast to a human purpose,
while spots of rust, below,
seep into concrete, eat and seek
return into the crazing stone.
Taken and forged of earth,
it is through dissolution to its source
that fence prepares to go…

In parts, the edges of this elevating path
have broken off and fallen to the lawn below.
There where the path was out of touch with earth,
laid over gaps of undulating ground,
or where, perhaps, the soil itself retracted,
and drew its grip from concrete,
the stress of unsupported human work
collapses back exhausted to the grass.

Adjacent here, that stretch of road
affirms the sum of human ingenuity,
its law and order, art and science,
the language that defines them all
but cannot it itself define;
that road that is in any sense all roads
in its projecting reach of space to space
and goal to goal from sign to sign,
unfolding as it does a causal code
of sequential circularity,
and yet is nothing more than just this road
in its particular here and now.

Its cracked and crusty double lines,
a mind's would-be eternal signs
eroded here like bits of dirty icing,
sink back from spheres of neat stability
to earthing's raw, corrosive undefined;
across the centre of that road the snaking crack
that severs cleanly through those lines
and clears a way for sprouting vegetation,
affirms the site where earthing and
ideal abstractions divide.

Dark emissaries of earth, those ceaseless ants,
emerge from holes and gaps. Black dots of code,
they form the lines of inscrutable ciphers,
run down the gutters and across a drain
where, clumped between its grate,
a host of weeds still somehow lodge
and flourish over an impossible abyss.
Those ants that harvest seeds and bits of leaf,
and claim for earth what earthing sheds
and leaves, discards or yields.

The sound of digging scuffs the air.
An elderly woman in a floral dress
crouched on her knees attends her garden.
She pauses, rests her hands upon her lap,
and through a web between two trees,
in which her face is perfectly framed,
shields her gaze and casts a smile this way.

Farther on, the leaves upon the path,
the brilliant red of bottlebrush stamens
filling in its gaps and cracks,
appear as if some master's hand
had set an ancient script
into a beautifully bordered design.
And floating on this work of chance suggesting order,
an image, a lingering image abides –

it is that woman in her floral dress
attending to her ordered garden
seen through that dew-dashed web,
the dirt lodged in beneath her nails,
the moist rich soil and sandy grains
still clinging to her fingers,
her smile, that face,
the earthing on her hands.

Kinetic Vision

My seeing, carried by a crow,
took flight, slipped through a leap to launch
in air, segueing from ascent
and glide to slur a lopped descent

atop a tree. From that black fluff
of feathers, perching as a stare,
two glancing eyes looked out to sea,
saw from the dancing wrack and sparkles

glancing there the sea look back…

Barbecue

In decorous conversation mixed
of quaint philosophy and liquor,
the made-up faces in the neat
backyard of formal, perfect premises
assume the poise and platitudes
of a groggily loved humanity.

Digesting palatable opinions
'round generously laden tables,
displaying each in civil tongues
and proper self-composing prose
the merely mirrored, they exchange
concordant geniality.

But just beneath the skulking sight
of that strange land of I, unsayable,
a veering shift of deviant looking
trespasses through the gloam of cloaked
invisibility to trail
dark-scented logics in the scrub –

there where the creature Reason lifts
a double-head and pining through
the tracts of tufted foliage on
its unrequited track sets forth
in hunger's cramped meander with
its sinuously stealthy strides.

In canopies of leafy dusk,
it primes taut sinews for their lunge
and crouching in its covert – lies.
Voracious, with dilated eyes
and tensing passion, it prepares
to pounce upon unwary prey

and with a swift, devouring vision,
(whose lusted blood and love are one,
as are coy grins and gleaming fangs)
dismember in its secret lair
of inconsolable alienation,
a phantom image of itself.

Emerging from its den one vision
faces another, wonders with
a fleeting thought, as soon forgot,
what hidden ghosts or panting beast
might lie behind that other's eyes.
With gracious smiles across a table

a plate of meat and salad's passed
by one deferring hand to another
amid the fizz of opened beers
and friendly pop of uncorked wine,
and then the searching talk resumes –
of ethics, politics, being and time.

Seagull (Exiting Parliament Station Underground)

for Malachi Doyle

Just barely born into the light
and smiling girls already hand
out glossy ads for something you
apparently need. The gift you pass
up with the same faux smile as theirs
is emphasised in bold print – 'Free!'

Across the road is Charles George Gordon
imperturbably transfixed.
Resting his foot on a shattered cannon,
steadfastly facing carnage with
indomitable poise, his pose
is redolent of the pure heroic…

But on his head, in an attitude
as fixed as his, a seagull peers
down Spring Street in the opposite
direction. Quaintly low-key in its
oblivious, non-heroic stance,
untouched by human need for mask

or myth, that seagull's gaze transcends
his show with genuine grace. 'What's on
its mind?' you think. 'Another gull,
or its next meal? Or just the fact
it's there and feels the stiffening breeze?'
Gladly, no human being can say.

You loosen with a fleeting mirth,
an honest smirk for that meek bird
that seems to say, 'Yes, it's absurd,
all this, you're all absurd but me!'
For something free that still exists,
you love that gull on Gordon's head…

Play

Let's say I'm one
and you are one –
together we make two,
then what could stand
between us ones
to make this sum untrue?

For ones to flow
into a two
there's nothing to say 'nay',
from two to three
and three to four
and any number's way.

So what permits
a difference here
to separate – or team – us
is just the way
we play at ones
when nothing lies between us.

Now take us two,
or any one,
divide each endlessly,
each fraction must
itself traverse
that nothing seamlessly.

By nothing then
are we denied
a meeting – you and me,
but rather by
what is no sum
we ones allowed to be;

which begs the question,
dearest love,
if through that passage – free,
before your face
I glean the grace
to glimpse infinity!

Monolith

For an intimacy of soul they felt
beyond their tactile reach
the lovers pressed each other close
to blot their bodily breach.

That love might stand in space conjoined,
and palpable as stone,
they yielded to a molten passion
to fuse again as one.

For surely distance could be spanned
and then that vast abyss
might shrink until it softly closed
to vanish in a kiss.

Yet braced to reach that perfect state,
still breathless and unsated,
they, gasping for each urgent kiss,
each other suffocated…

Glory days

These summery suburban streets that lie
deserted, thick with silence, are like a bland
and barely conscious mind – expressionless
and hazy in their distant vacancy;

bare lifeless streets that waste in the sun,
anonymously withdrawn and empty of
the ring of laughing children as they ride
their bikes or tussle for a lusted ball…

Abandoned playgrounds overgrown, where have
they gone, and what seductive piper wooed
them from our midst into his sunless land?
Do they in those sepulchral caskets ranged

in lines, their curtains drawn to block daylight's
intrusive glare, sit gravely fixed in front
of televisions or computer screens
immersed in lonely heroics and virtual realms?

From somewhere distant, suddenly, I hear
the backyard-cricket whack of bat and ball,
hear urgent screams excite the air as up-
turned eyes and arms, ascended in their poise,

await the fateful end of willow's smack
to captured eager catch or fumbled fall,
see flitting bodies swiftly glide aloft,
for one ecstatic moment soar, then arc

and tumble down with sliding grunts to earth –
in open air and gorgeous dirt, scuffed knees
and elbows proudly worn like battle scars,
they triumph in each other's praising gaze.

With mutual admiration and esteem,
their bodies ripe with achievement's ache
and wholesome tang of sweat upon their lips,
they wend a weary way to home and tea.

But wending wearily to me, the here-and-now
returned from memory, I wonder if
a kid inside those boxes, washed and groomed
with over-indulgent care and sterile worry,

sits there mechanically tapping at
his keyboard, silently transfixed upon
a screen, his body cramped with eyes fatigued
amid the fetid air, distracted by

the useless pot-plant on his desk, aware
it's there when it obstructs his mousse, for which
he'd dump the thing outside, but which his mum
insists so lends his room a natural touch.

Celebrity

I con you with a smile of bleached-white teeth,
my sculpted hair and sparkling touched-up eyes,
I con you with endearing skill, a thief,
who leaves you wanting more of his sweet lies.
I con you with the aura of my fame,
the dark self-love your nescience vests in me,
I con you with the ideal life I feign
which screens the inner emptiness you flee.
I con you with the idealising dreams
within whose night your light expires,
I con you all with this – what merely seems,
the blind projections of your own desires;
so, worship this, the masking surface I don,
you on your knees before me here – an icon.

Nascent

The earth is billions of years old,
so clocking science plainly chimes,
but set aside all human scales,
then it's still in its birthing time;

for should you take infinity,
divide it over, times untold,
each fraction of that span would merge
as one eternal-whole-day old.

Now we, we know, are civilised,
reflective souls with brains to suit,
but just attend yourself in sleep
and there you'll meet a primal brute.

Yet man's the marvel of the world,
conceit so tells a coddled pet,
but man's just still a grand idea
to which we've not arrived at yet.

Villanelle

Though chance obstructs us with disruptive might
to thwart and hold our coupling goal apart,
do we as fated lovers finally unite?

Our constant purpose spreads before our sight
as does the course ordained before we start,
though chance obstructs us with disruptive might.

Invoke a cosmos of discordant spite –
a chaos that withholds harmonic parts –
do we as fated lovers finally unite?

While Cupid's aim is fraught with blinded flight,
ours is no random whim or errant dart,
though chance obstructs us with disruptive might.

Since sceptics doubt a rhyme as something slight
when no caprice diverts our sterner art –
do we as fated lovers finally unite?

Let soul despair of sense in nescient night,
a couplet sings with one conjoining heart:
'Though chance obstructs us with disruptive might,
we do as fated lovers finally unite!'

The Fanatic

Beneath the fervour of his fiery eye –
the righteous rhetoric of his baying rage –
each empty sound he ululates belies
what no convulsive raving can assuage.
The more he babbles of his holy heights
the vaster gapes the chasm at his feet,
the more of heart he makes a block of ice,
then by as much his zeal devoid of heat.
A Narcissus seduced by his own visage
he sets his grotesque idol up as God,
demanding others bow before his image
or risk its petty wrath of lusted blood –
an outward show, each shout of faith without,
within a maniac masking his self-doubt.

Impossible Love

A heaviness of heart is like a setting sun,
its splendour lavished with dissembled pride;
for all its outward show and pompous gloss,
the sumptuous guise of ripeness in its run
as it declines with ease to eventide,
the longing shadows moan of looming loss…
Walking alone in the sweet-scented night,
my heart's that sunken sun concealed from sight,
and in my long and solitary round
oppressed and silent in the cloudy gloom,
a luminescent skewer pierces through
the night, an ache as soon obscurely drowned
and veiled like light beneath the mantled moon –
this love I feel for any thought of you.

www.ingramcontent.com/pod-product-compliance
Lightning Source LLC
Chambersburg PA
CBHW070050120526
44589CB00034B/1710